5 Steps to Lasting LOVE

An Evidence-based Guide to Protecting & Repairing Your Relationship

ANN MARIE TAYLOR

HG Dip (P), BA (hons), MHGI, MBPsS

First edition 2019

Published by Brainheart Publishing & Ann Marie Taylor, November 2019

Cover Art and Interior Design:
Heidi Sutherlin www.mycreativepursuits.com

DISCLAIMER:

The advice and strategies found within may not be suitable for every situation; in particular, this book is not intended for people in abusive relationships who are advised to seek professional help.

This work is sold with the understanding that neither the author nor the publisher will be held responsible for the results accrued from the advice in this book.

Praise for

5 Steps to Lasting Love

The Missing Relationship Instruction

Tim Ebl

This book should be handed out with every marriage license! It's loaded with easy to understand steps that anyone can start using immediately in any relationship. I learned a lot- both about what I need to focus more on, as well as some things I am doing right already and have to keep up. I really think this information is the key to a lasting, living relationship and will be getting copies of this book to give to my children.

Well written, interesting and extremely useful. Love it!

A Jewel of a book with Evidenced Based and Heart Felt Advice!

Kim Mowatt

I have been a Registered Psychiatric Nurse and counsellor for 35 years, and I will definitely recommend this manual to my clients! Simple, and easy to follow evidence base advice, it is wonderful! I especially liked" A problem-focused approach increases the emotional arousal—making it more difficult for everyone to see the big picture and get a perspective on what they are trying to achieve, a loving supportive relationship and a culture of appreciation." It is so important to focus on what is going well, and I love this in the message of this jewel of a book.

Practical, straightforward advice

John A. Weiler

If you are struggling in your relationship, then this book will help pull you of your rut, set you back on track, and start building a loving relationship.

The best part about this book to me is how incredibly simple, practical, and easy to follow the advice is.

You can pick up this book, read it in a day, and start implementing the actionable advice this evening. The author provides case studies from her practice and these clearly show her ability to improve couples' relationships using the techniques in this book.

Whether your relationship is falling apart or is doing well, there is something here for everyone in this book. Read this book, and your relationship will improve. It's as simple as that!

DOWNLOAD THE AUDIOBOOK

FOR FREE!

Just to say *thank you* for buying my book, I would like to give you the audiobook version 100% FREE!

To download your free copy go to:

www.greystonescounselling.ie/free-audiobook

Contents

"A loving atmosphere in your home
is the foundation of your life."

—The Dalai Lama

For want of a nail the shoe was lost.
For want of a shoe the horse was lost.
For want of a horse the rider was lost.
For want of a rider the message was lost.
For want of a message the battle was lost.
For want of a battle the kingdom was lost.
And all for the want of a horseshoe nail.

—Proverb

Introduction

In modern life, many people struggle to make their relationships work. The health of our most important relationship can impact on all areas of our lives, including on our physical health, our levels of stress and anxiety, our finances, and our ability to focus at work.

In fact, a 75 years long, ongoing research project has found that the biggest predictor of long-term happiness and longevity is the quality of our personal relationships.[1]

This book is for anyone who would like to understand how to make a relationship work in the long-term.

It is also for people in a long-term relationship that once worked but is now in distress. It aims not only to help you put things right—but also to equip you with the knowledge and skills to strengthen and protect it, and make things work in the long haul.

My own experience from years of working as a psychotherapist with both couples and individuals, is that when even just one partner puts in the effort to really understand and follow the principles in this book, it is often possible to alter the whole dynamic and turn things around.

Having said that, it is also of course the case that prevention is always better than cure; in other words, the sooner you take action the more likely your chances of success.

My purpose in writing this book is to give individuals who are experiencing a relationship crisis or are just concerned about the way things are going, a clear guide as to what they can do that will really make a difference.

Using the methods described here, I have been able to help even some couples who came to me on the verge of splitting up—thinking it was probably too late—to find and reconnect with each other again.

I have seen couples go from saying that they have not slept together for years or that their partner is throwing them out, to holding hands, enjoying family days out with their kids, sleeping together, and rekindling their romance, often within six to twelve weeks.

If your relationship is in difficulty, this book will give you a clear plan of action for reducing tension and getting things back on track.

Don't let your most important relationship fail through a lack of effort!

The steps and tips that you are about to read, have helped many people to create positive, long-lasting change in their relationships.

I bumped into a client whom I hadn't seen for three months, a couple of weeks ago. He had been close to splitting up with his partner, though he loved her very much. "I've been meaning to come and tell you," he said, "All that stuff you told me about relationships—it worked! I couldn't believe it! I am amazed!"

So, if what you want is to repair or improve a relationship that once (maybe long ago) was good, but is difficult now, you have come to the right place!

So, what are you waiting for?

Dive right in and start creating and enjoying the relationship and home life you deserve.

Why I am Writing this Book

About twenty-eight years ago, when I was an under-graduate studying psychology, I first came across the research on which I've expanded in this book. At that time, it had no relevance to my own life, so although it was interesting, I didn't give it much thought.

Years later, when I'd been with my husband about seven years, I came across a book prominently displayed in the library, named The Relationship Cure by John Gottman. I recognised him as a psychologist who, at that time, had done about thirty years of research on relationships and was world-leading in this area.

I decided to read it, out of professional, academic interest.

Although by this time, we had been having frequent rows, I didn't really think that there was any cause for concern in my own relationship. However, as soon as I began reading the book, I became alarmed!

It was clear to me, within a few chapters, that my own marriage was in danger. The world's foremost authority on relationships, Professor John Gottman, was predicting that my own relationship would end in breakdown—and worse—the implication of what he was saying, was that this would be my fault!

I was horrified and vowed to change my behaviour immediately. I managed to do so (though like changing any bad habits—it was not easy) and continued to apply the lessons I'd learned to my own relationship.

Several years later, having trained in a modern solution-focused form of psychotherapy, Human Givens Therapy, and having immersed myself further in Gottman's research, I started applying what I'd learned to my work with clients.

I found that by combining a solution-focused approach with some of Gottman's key findings, I was often also able to help my clients to turn around their relationships, too. This was sometimes the case, even when the state of their relationship was extreme.

Even when all seemed lost, whether they came alone or with their partner, it was often possible to help people to turn things around completely, so that they became a supportive, loving team again.

Therefore, I decided to write this book. It seems to me that some of the most important findings of Gottman's research have been lost, in the sense that people "can't see the wood for the trees."

In the mass of information available to people searching for help in the internet age, some of the most important findings are not "out there" in a way that is easy to understand and put into practice.

It also seems to me that attempts to help couples in distress are often failing unnecessarily because the implications of some of the research seem to have been missed, even by the professionals.

So, if your relationship is in difficulty or even has reached breaking point, but you still want to make things work, this book is for you!

I hope this book will help you to go back to how you used to be, to how you'd like to be again: a loving, caring, team having fun together and supporting each other through life's journey and through the many challenges you will undoubtedly face.

Because love is a journey that can lead to riches greater than gold...

Step One

Get the Basics Right

Chapter 1

The Three Behaviours that Heal

"Things that matter most must never be at the mercy of things that matter least."

—Johann Wolfgang von Goethe

Research shows that there are three key behaviours that make a relationship work long-term. I call them the behaviours that heal. They are the foundation of a healthy relationship.

At the start of a relationship, everybody does these things.

At the start of the relationship, we are often "in love" or at least really into the other person. We spend a lot of time together; talking, touching, and bonding.

That's why, at the start, none of us have problems with communication.

When we're getting the little things right, both partners feel valued, supported, and cared for, and that gives both partners positive expectations of each other and of the relationship. That is why we get along so well in the early days.

But as a relationship goes on, people tend to go back to their old patterns of being busy. The little things start to be neglected and bad habits develop.

Let's be clear: nobody knows that these things are important! This is part of the problem; it is why I am writing this book.

Unfortunately, what happens is that this neglect of the little things causes a cascade of negative effects. These lead to many of the most common difficulties that people experience in relationships.

It was found, for example, that affairs usually came after, rather than before this process of breakdown. The research is clear that problems commonly start with very small things going wrong.

That's the bad news. The good news is that when you know this and what those small things that matter are and focus on getting them right, it is my experience that the relationship can often be turned around.

To be clear, I'm not saying that this is the cause of all relationship problems or that this is the only thing that matters. What I am saying is that, in most cases, this is where you need to start to effectively repair the damage between you.

These little things build and become the foundation of a relationship that works.

If you do these simple, but all-important things first, then it will be much easier for you to talk about your difficulties and work through them, either together or with professional help.

But until you are getting these things right, any other attempts to address your difficulties are less likely to work, because you will both be too hurt and/or angry to listen to your partner properly.

A renewed focus on getting the basics right, is a necessary first step to rebuilding the trust in each other.

This can start to bring down the levels of criticism, defensiveness, and contempt that usually flood a relationship in difficulty and that stand in the way of overcoming your problems.

Remember:

Getting the little things right is like oiling the cogs of the relationship—over time, everything else becomes much easier.

The No. 1 behaviour that harms

Many years ago, before I was a therapist, a couple I was friendly with split up. They both came separately to see me and tell me their side of the story. It was a very messy split with a lot of anger, affairs, and recriminations. But underlying all of this, it seemed to me, that both had the same fundamental complaint: that the other partner wasn't giving them enough attention.

The man's main complaint was that the woman would never look up from her laptop when he came home from work and wanted to talk to her about his day. The woman's main grievance was that the TV took up so much of his attention, that she felt like throwing it out of the window.

This was an "Ah ha!" moment for me—I thought, "Gottman is right! This disastrous split that looks at first glance to be about affairs, is really about attention and failed bids for connection!"

Attention is the water of love.

(A plant—before and after water. Photos by W. Fricke)

So, what are these three behaviours that heal?

Well, the first one is attention. I call attention the water of love, because research shows that attention is a crucial factor in relationships.

We all need attention, but unfortunately, modern life steals our attention. All the present-day gadgets—phones, the TV, game stations—together with our very busy, modern patterns of working, compete for our already-limited attention.

Unfortunately, the behaviour that is most harmful to a relationship is almost certainly not giving your partner enough of your attention; specifically, not listening to them.

Let's unpack that a bit—what are we really talking about here?

We are talking about giving your partner an opportunity to talk about the seemingly "trivial" everyday stuff that may be completely boring to you.

It is boring to everyone else, too! That is the point. Because this stuff is not intrinsically interesting, probably the most essential role of a partner (if he or she wants a happy relationship, long-term, anyway) is to listen to this stuff.

Here are some examples of the sort of topics we're talking about:

- The dog's operation;
- A programme that was on TV last night;
- What we are having for dinner;
- My sister's choice of outfit for the wedding;
- The cat's health;
- My co-worker's habit of picking her nails;

- Whether we should have the radiator in the bathroom replaced;
- Et cetera.

So not-sexy, interesting stuff...

Giving your partner daily opportunities to share the things that are on their mind—the things that they're concerned about, because it is important to them—(even if it is boring to you) is essential to the long-term health of your relationship.

And what is hugely important to your partner (to anyone's partner) is the chance to share this stuff— to offload or vent, anything that is on their mind or affecting them emotionally.

And this one action—listening to your partner talk about the things that they want to talk about (and finding ways to show that you are listening!)—has the most potential to make your partner feel loved, cared for, and supported. It is as crucial as that!

If you don't do it, it also has the greatest potential to make your partner feel unloved, uncared for, and unsupported.

Yes, that is right: you read that right! This one behaviour will make more difference than anything else you do to make your partner feel loved or unloved! It is as powerful and important as that!

When John Gottman and his team talked to people who were being regularly ignored or blocked in their attempts to talk to their partners and asked them how they felt about it, they were amazed at the level of hurt and the degree of harm that was being done, usually unwittingly.

These were not, on the face of it, “important” conversations; they might have wanted to talk about the cat’s food, the football results, or some gossip at work. In other words, ordinary, everyday stuff.

But when their partner was too busy with something else to listen to them, they felt hurt, neglected, and unloved. They felt ignored, as though their concerns were unimportant to their partner.

Gottman and his team were amazed at how short a time elapsed between being on the receiving end of this behaviour and stopping trying altogether to capture a partner’s attention.

Not surprisingly, this would then lead to the second stage of a relationship’s deterioration. At this stage, at least one partner would start experiencing very negative thoughts about the other.

Giving your partner opportunities to talk about their day, the stuff that is on their mind and letting them know that you are listening is the best way of making them feel loved, supported, and cared for.

To me, it is clear from the research that meeting this need is one of the most important roles of a partner.

If you are achieving this, you are well on the way to having a successful relationship, but if you are not, no matter how great a partner you are in other ways, it will all count for nothing—unfair as that may seem!

So, the research found that when this wasn't happening, the partner on the receiving end felt ignored, unloved, and uncared for.

The partner doing the ignoring usually didn't realise that they were doing something wrong. They weren't aware that what they were doing was having a hugely detrimental effect on their relationship.

And the researchers found that the person on the receiving end of being ignored would stop trying to engage with the other person. They would stop trying to get them to listen to what was on their mind—and this would happen quickly.

Instead of doing that, the second person would now withdraw from their partner and start to see them in a very negative light.

They would feel hurt, they would feel unloved, they would feel angry... and the psychologists doing this research were amazed by how quickly someone who was failing to obtain their partner's attention when they looked for it, would stop trying.

The Research

When John Gottman started his life's work in the 1970s, no-one really knew what made relationships work or break down; the research just hadn't been done.

Human nature being what it is, that did not stop people setting themselves up as "experts" in the field and at that time, the leading theory was that people in great relationships were good at self-disclosure. It was this openness and communication that was thought to explain their successful relationships.

This theory is still very prevalent, despite not being based on research. It just seems to make sense to a lot of people.

Gottman thought—like everyone else—that the theory was probably right and expected to find lots of self-disclosure and long conversations about the relationship, in the relationships that worked.

But that wasn't what they found.

So, at first, they thought, "Are we doing something wrong?" They kept refining and improving their research methods.[2]

But whatever they did, nobody seemed to be having these great in-depth conversations about themselves and their relationship.

Eventually, John Gottman said (to paraphrase), "Okay, the theory is wrong. We need to go back to our data and see if we can find out what's really happening; see if we can find any patterns."

What they did find was that some people were having hugely successful, fulfilling relationships and that others weren't. They also found that everybody seemed to be having lots of very trivial conversations about seemingly not very much at all.

But it turned out that these "trivial" conversations were in fact hugely important and that there was a pattern to them. That pattern predicted whether the relationship would work or fail in the long term. They were as crucial as that!

The pattern was that one partner would try and get the other person's attention, which John Gottman called a "bid for connection." They could do this in many ways, such as with a gesture, a question, a look, a touch—any single expression that said, "I want to feel connected to you."

So, for example, one bid for connection might be, "Would you like a cup of tea?" and the person on the receiving end of that could reply in one of three ways.

1) Turning towards

So, the first way might be, "No, thank you."

Now, although the person said no, they answered the question and successfully connected, and so that was counted as a positive interaction and they called that "turning towards".

2) Turning away

If the other person is busy watching the TV or scrolling through their phone or something, they may fail to respond at all. Researchers called this failure to connect "turning away".

Another form of that might be, responding to the same question with, "Did I tell you that your sister rang?"

Since that response is not relevant to the question asked, it is still a failure to connect. That would again be turning away.

3) Turning against

A third type of response would be, "You think that would make everything alright, do you?" Researchers called this type of negative, insulting, or critical response "turning against".

What they found was that too much turning away and turning against predicted the end of the relationship. "Husbands headed for divorce disregard their wife's bid for connection 82% of the time, while husbands in stable relationships disregard their wives' bids just 19% of the time." (The corresponding figures for wives were 50% versus 14%).[3]

What really surprised the researchers was how hurt and upset the person on the receiving end of a failed bid for connection was, and how quickly they stopped trying to get their partner's attention at all.

For example, it may be that your partner is hugely interested in rugby and you may not be interested in rugby at all. Even if that is the case, it's massively important that you let your partner talk to you about the rugby, particularly if they have no one else to hand who shares their enthusiasm for it. They may not have anyone else they can talk to about this, or no one else they can share this with on a daily basis.

I know it is not easy. When we are fully focused on something else—reading, watching TV, or whatever—our attention is locked.[4] It is very hard when your attention is locked in this way to put the phone down or turn away from the TV and give your partner your full attention.

And of-course, it is not always possible or appropriate for us to do this. We may need to say, "Sorry, I'm just in the middle of something here. Can we talk about this later?"

But then make sure that you do make a point of getting back to them to talk about it. It is so important to the long-term health of your relationship that you make the time and the effort to do this.

The truth is this:

These little daily things matter and some of them are crucial.

Probably the most important of those "little things" is giving your partner the gift of your full attention—not necessarily even for huge amounts of time—but more often in little bursts when our partner is asking for it.

We underestimate the importance of this at our peril!

The best research in this area has shown that it is the little things in a relationship that mount up over time and either destroy it by undermining its foundations or turn it into the rock solid, close and life-long friendship that most of us want to achieve.

So, for example, a man feeling unloved and uncared for (because his partner is failing to meet his need for attention) might look at the towels his partner has dumped on the bathroom floor and say to himself, "Look she's done it again! How many more times do I have to ask her to hang them up! It just shows that she doesn't care about me... If she did, she would remember that this is important to me! How hard can it be to pick up a towel?"

This man may then conclude that his dissatisfaction with the relationship is because his partner is untidy and inconsiderate and refuses to change. And, of course, it is important to do your best to change habits that are annoying to your partner.

However, if this man was getting his essential, innate need for attention met within the relationship, the likelihood is that he would be more forgiving of her faults. The towel problem would just not bug him so much.

When we are feeling emotionally distressed, neuroscience[5] shows that our emotions are in charge, and our thinking brain (neocortex) shuts down, reducing our ability to think clearly. (This is why people say, "I can't think straight").

So, in this emotional state of feeling unloved and uncared for, people start thinking about their partners in a very negative way. They start thinking "s/he doesn't love me, s/he doesn't care for me, s/he doesn't give a damn."

They start focusing on all the things that their partners are doing wrong, on all the things that they feel unhappy about. They feel ignored, unloved, and uncared for. And every little thing that their partner does wrong or doesn't do, becomes magnified, and all the many, many things that their partners might be doing right, count for nothing.

These thoughts then spill out into criticism and hurtful comments that, in turn, leave their partner feeling unloved and uncared for. The partner now becomes defensive.

Little by little, the home starts to turn into a war zone with each partner growing in hostility towards the other and each increasingly having negative expectations of their partner and of the relationship.

I recently asked an older man, a widow who had enjoyed a long and happy marriage what he thought the most important ingredient was, to make a relationship work. He thought long and hard and then said, "Listening."

Not listening enough is alone predictive of relationship breakdown.[6] If there is only one thing that you take from this book and apply to your relationship—and indeed, to all the relationships that are important to you—I hope it is this!

Chapter summary

- Attention is the water of love.
- Regularly listening to your partner talk, about whatever is on their mind, is essential to protect the long-term health of your relationship.
- The things that your partner wants to talk about, may not seem important or interesting to you, but your role as their partner is to listen.

- Probably the most important, protective thing that you can do for your relationship is, at least some of the time, ideally every day, stop anything else you are doing; put away the phone, turn off the TV—and really listen to your partner—even if it's just for five or ten minutes.

Chapter 2

The First Pattern of Relationship Breakdown

The most common pattern of relationship breakdown is escalating conflict. The partners start rowing more; insulting each other, shouting at each other, and the rows become increasingly frequent and serious.

Now, an interesting thing that the research found is that all relationships have conflict. Some people have great relationships and get on well, but those relationships also have conflict.

So, to be clear, it is not that arguments in themselves are bad—they can be helpful in clearing the air—it is conflict that is getting more frequent and severe that is a cause for concern.

The difference between relationships that work well, and ones that are in difficulty is that in those that work long-term, the conflict tends to fizzle out quickly. This seems to be a key difference between relationships that work and relationships that don't.

So, the researchers looked at, why does this happen? Why is it that in some relationships, conflict fizzles out quickly and in other relationships, it worsens?

What they found was that in all conflicts, one person would make what they called a repair attempt—an attempt to bring the conflict to an end. The repair attempt would either work (in which case the conflict would end) or it would not work, in which case the row would escalate.

Repair attempts that work, turned out to be one of the biggest predictors of a relationships long-term success.

They found that repair attempts could take many forms, including smiling, time out, an apology, a joke, or a gesture of affection.

Whether a repair attempt works or not seems to be the key factor in whether a row escalates or fizzles out. So, a central question became: what makes a repair attempt successful or unsuccessful?

The first thing the researchers looked at was how good the person—making the repair attempt was at communicating; how eloquent, sophisticated, and competent they were in their attempt to repair the damage.

Surprisingly, they found that this wasn't a factor at all. Someone could make a fantastically competent and sophisticated repair attempt and it would fail. Their partner wouldn't seem to hear it or wouldn't respond to it and the conflict would just continue to become worse.

By contrast they found that someone else could make a clumsy, inept, and seemingly incompetent attempt to bring the conflict to an end, and it would work! Their partner would hear it, respond to it, and the conflict would end. So, whatever the key factor was, it was not the competence of the attempt.

They had to look for other factors to explain the difference between a repair attempt that works and one that fails.

This was crucial information, because it was the key to whether the conflict escalated, which often led to relationship breakdown or whether the conflict fizzled out quickly, which is what was happening in relationships that worked.

They eventually discovered that the crucial aspect was the quality of the friendship with the partner before the conflict. In other words, how loved, cared for and supported the person on the receiving end of the repair attempt felt before the conflict started.

If Partner A and Partner B were in a row and B felt loved, supported, and cared for before the row broke out, then s/he would hear any repair attempt Partner A made and it would work.

Even if the repair attempt was clumsy and unsophisticated, it would work.

So, the crucial factor turned out to be how loved and supported the other person felt by their partner before the row.

The million-dollar question now is: What makes a partner feel loved and supported?

The answer to that is the three behaviours that heal: attention (listening), affection, and focusing on the positive (appreciation).

Chapter summary

- Escalating conflict is the main pattern of relationship breakdown.
- All relationships have conflict.
- In relationships that work long-term, conflict fizzles out quickly because repair attempts are heard.
- Whether a repair attempt is heard or not depends solely on how loved, cared for, and supported the person it is aimed at felt before the conflict.
- We can best make our partner feel loved and supported with the three behaviours that heal: attention, affection, and focusing on the positive.
- When our partner feels loved and supported conflicts become more likely to blow over quickly.

Chapter 3

The Second Pattern of Relationship Breakdown

The second most common pattern of relationship breakdown is were a couple doesn't have many rows; they just drift apart. They become strangers to one another, because they lose their emotional connection.

The research has clearly found that this occurs over time, due to a lack of expressions of affection. People simply lose the habit of showing affection to each other.

There may not be any open conflict; instead, they become like "ships that pass in the night" as they increasingly live separate lives.

These are the couples we see sitting in restaurants and not talking—they have nothing to say to each other.

So, the second behaviour that heals, is gestures of affection.

In the beginning of a relationship, couples give each other a lot of attention and affection. They do this all the time in thousands of little smiles, gestures, touches, and kind words. This is completely normal and happens constantly in the first weeks and months of a relationship—words of appreciation, touches, smiles, squeezes of the shoulder, hugs, and kisses are exchanged all the time.

Unfortunately, as time goes on, this starts to happen less. We tend to go back to the pattern of our life before the relationship—our usual busy patterns of working hard and trying to relax, by walking the dog, watching the telly, keeping fit, or all the other things with which people fill their time.

In all this rushing about; all this dealing with the daily struggles and challenges of life, we just get out of the habit of doing the things that really matter.

Again, the message of just how important this is, is not written as large in the world as it should be. People just don't know it is important!

Because most people don't know that being affectionate to our nearest and dearest is hugely important, it is often one of the first things to go, along with listening.

It's easy to get out of the habit of doing these simple, daily things, but they really can make all the difference.

And once you are out of the habit, of course, it all starts to feel very strange and unnatural. It can be awkward to start making gestures of affection again, after a long time of not doing so.

So, if you recognise yourself and your partner in this description, start small.

Start building little gestures of affection back into your relationship. You might start with a touch of the hand, a squeeze of the shoulder, a kiss of the forehead, or a few words of appreciation about the things your partner is doing right, or the things you like about them.

Wherever you start, you need to start somewhere.

Failure to express affection can be just a bad habit that you have developed over time, but like any bad habit, it will need effort to overcome and to change it.

Gestures of affection are bound to feel unnatural at first, if you have been out of the habit of doing these things for a long time.

The good news is that, like all the things we learn or must relearn, it becomes easier the more often we do it. But expect it to be hard at first.

So, start small and build up!

Start with little things: little squeezes of the hand or touches of the arm.

A word of warning!

When you start doing this, your partner might throw it all back in your face! They might say:

"You just got this out of that book, didn't you? You don't really mean it! You don't really care! You are just doing what it says in that stupid book! Did you think I would fall for that rubbish! I wonder how long you can keep this up for?"

They might really do their best to make this difficult for you!

Understand that, if they do this it is because they are hurt and angry. They have probably been feeling neglected and taken for granted for a long time and they don't want to be taken for a fool and hurt again.

Rome wasn't built in a day!

So, what can you do?

Keep on keeping on!

Accept that this is likely to be the case. Commit now to following the plan in this book for at least forty days.

Give it your best shot and see what happens! Refuse to take their negativity personally!

Accept that your partner's negativity about your new-found affection is a consequence of your previous neglect.

I am not saying it is your fault—you were busy earning a crust, keeping a roof over your head, ensuing the kids were clean and fed—it's easy to overlook these things with all modern life's demands for our attention.

But however, you do it, make sure that you do; because the research clearly shows that these gestures of affection can mean the world to your partner.

Over time, they are what makes us feel emotionally connected to one another. If we fail to do these things, irritation and annoyance with each other's little habits can start to grow like weeds in the fertile ground of neglect.

We become like strangers, because we have lost something very important: our emotional connection to each other.

The research shows us that the cause of this tragedy is lack of expressions of affection. It's not necessarily a lack of affection, but the failure to express it in a way that the other person can feel it.

This is what people really mean when they say, "we have grown apart".

So, don't let it happen to you!

If it has already happened, take heart; it may not be too late.

It is possible to recover from these situations. Relationships are a dynamic; in my experience, if one person starts to change their behaviour, very often, the whole dynamic starts to shift.

Have you ever seen a plate of ice crack, or film of an ice shelf breaking off?

It can look as though nothing is happening. On the surface everything stays the same, but then, suddenly, it just breaks—more quickly than you think...

Relationship repair can be like this too, but it needs effort from at least one partner—day after day, for weeks or months—to really turn things around.

And all the while it may look as if nothing is happening and, on the surface, things may stay the same, for weeks or months.

Until one day—the ice breaks...

There is a famous historical example of how important attention and affection are to us.[7]

According to the Italian historian and monk Salimbene di Ada, Holy Roman Emperor Frederick II, in the 13th century, was interested in finding out what language children would speak if they never heard any speech.

To achieve this, Frederick II had several babies (the exact number wasn't recorded) brought up by nurses. The nurses were under strict instructions to keep the babies clean and fed, and to look after them in all the usual ways, except that they were not allowed to talk to them or to touch them any more then was strictly necessary. They were just to do what was essential to keep them alive.

Unfortunately, Frederick never received an answer to his question, because tragically, all the babies brought up without attention and affection, died as infants. Salimbene di Ada reported that they 'could not live without petting".

Chapter summary

- The second-most common pattern of relationship breakdown is growing apart.
- Partners become like strangers although they aren't necessarily having any rows.
- Research shows that this is caused by not regularly expressing affection to each other.
- Over time, a lack of affection leads to the loss of emotional connection.

Chapter 4

The Third Behaviour that Heals

A woman once told me about her husband and his bad behaviour which included things like making food and drinks for himself but never asking her if she wanted any, being only interested in money, being self-obsessed and messy and not helping with the housework. She said that he was a nightmare to live with and that she was thoroughly fed up with him and thinking about leaving.

I then asked her to tell me about his good side —tell me about what first attracted her to him. She was dismayed and said, “Do I have to?”

I said, “Yes you do.”

So, she told me how great he was with their three kids; she told me about his spiritual and ethical side, that first attracted her to him. She told me about his love of travel, about his intelligence and about the comfortable lifestyle that he was providing for them all with his high earning but demanding job.

It painted a completely different picture from the one that she had previously described!

This same thing has now happened to me many times.

I sometimes think that we could all paint a picture like that of our partner if we focused just on their bad side (& most of them would not have too much difficulty painting a similar picture of us if they tried)!

The third behaviour that heals is focusing on the positive.

As we’ve seen, relationship breakdowns often start with one person feeling neglected and unloved because they’re not receiving enough attention or affection. They then start to withdraw from the other person.

From this place of feeling hurt and unloved, they start to focus solely on the negatives in the relationship. They start to see only the things that the other person is doing wrong or not doing at all.

Unfortunately, when we are in that very emotional place where we are feeling hurt, unloved and neglected, our thinking brain—the neocortex—shuts down and we become trapped in the emotional part of our brain and unable to think clearly.

This is part of a survival mechanism that is in all of us and we can all react in this way.

When we are very emotional, our ability to think shuts down and however intelligent we usually are, emotion makes us behave foolishly. This has been described as the amygdala hijacking the thinking brain.[8]

So, because we are overly emotional, we cannot think clearly and, in this state, it is all too easy to focus only on the negatives—on what our partner is not doing, or on what they are doing wrong. We may fail to see any of the things that our partner is doing right.

By contrast, our partners may feel that they are putting a huge amount of effort into the relationship.

They may feel that they're great with the kids, cleaning the house, and/or are supporting their family by working hard and bringing in a good income. They may feel like they're doing a wonderful job as a partner and be oblivious to how we are feeling.

They may well be doing all these great things, but the partner who is feeling neglected, and is trapped in their emotions, sees only the things that the other person is not doing and that they are doing wrong.

This is a trap that we can all fall into, especially during a long relationship.

I myself am in a committed relationship of twenty-five years, and even now—of course—sometimes my partner will do things that annoy me (and I will do things that annoy him). This is normal in any relationship.

If I'm not careful, I can still easily be sucked into that negative mindset of focusing only on the things that annoy me and allowing them to drive me mad!

So, to avoid that, I "catch myself" when I find myself thinking in this way. I take a moment and remind myself of all the things that I appreciate about my partner, all the things that attracted me to him in the first place, and all the things that he is doing right.

We can all learn to do this; to stop the train of thought that focuses only on what our partner is doing wrong.

This is vital, because if we allow ourselves to go down that path, all our negative thoughts will start spilling out into the relationship as criticism.

This will then most likely lead to defensiveness from our partner and, before we know it, we will have created a toxic, negative atmosphere in our home.

Gottman's team found that some people are great at relationships. They called these couples The Masters and looked for what these couples are doing differently from the rest of us.

What they found was that these couples,[9] by contrast, manage to create a culture of appreciation and friendship in their homes and are gentle with each other. This is what we all need to aim for (however far off it may seem at the moment!).

In relationships, as in life, it is important to be careful about what you focus on. This can sound to some people like magical thinking, so I will explain it to you.

Our brains follow patterns, so the healthier and more positive the patterns we put into our brain, the more likely we are to achieve something close to the outcome we desire. Also, being optimistic about a positive outcome can motivate us to work harder to achieve it and being pessimistic can unfortunately lead to us unwittingly rehearsing failure (see for example the discussion of interview performance in Chapter 10, Rehearsing Success).

I will give you some more examples:

Example one

Think of a child who is behaving badly. Unfortunately, when the child behaves well, the parent, who is stressed and busy, is happy that the child is behaving well and so ignores the child to get on with other things. As a result, the child receives very little attention when he or she behaves well.

I am sure you can already see the pitfall here!

Suddenly, the child starts to misbehave. The parent is then immediately there, reacting to the bad behaviour, and in doing so, giving them their full attention.

Maybe the parent is shouting or maybe the parent is critical, but however negative the attention, it is still attention. And attention is a powerful thing.

We all need attention and any attention will do. So, even shouting and telling the child off, can make the behaviour we are focusing on more likely to happen again, particularly if the child is not getting any attention when they are behaving well...

The child will behave badly if that's the only way they can reliably receive some sort of interaction from the parent.

For this reason, raising a happy, well-behaved child is most easily achieved by praising and giving attention to, what the child is doing right.

Example two

The book In Search of Solutions[10] advocates a solution-focused approach in therapy and social work. It gives numerous examples of professionals' attempts to address a problem by focusing on the problem that unfortunately lead to the problem becoming worse.

There is also an example of this—the problem is focusing on the problem—in chapter 6, Common Problems in Communication.

So, as I said, in relationships, as in life, be careful what you focus on. This can be summed up as "What you focus on is what you get".

A Word of Warning

Focusing on the positive is not a "get out of jail free card" meaning that you don't have to listen to and act on your partner's complaints! The research is also clear that it is important to be influenced by your partner—in other words to listen to and consider what they say!

If your relationship is in difficulty, your partner's complaints are very often your best guide as to where you are going wrong. This may seem obvious, but I have been surprised how often people tell me that their family and friends have advised them to ignore their partner's complaints!

It's important, when making decisions in your relationship to be clear what your goal is and to stay focused on that. For most people I work with, their goal is to make their relationship work better and to put it on a more sustainable long-term footing.

When someone gives you advice about how you should behave with your partner, ask yourself—will what they are suggesting take me towards or further away from my goal?

I think it is also a good idea to look carefully at who is giving the advice and how happy their own relationships are! I have also been surprised at how often people are willing to take relationship advice from others who themselves have a long history of unhappy and broken relationships.

If you are looking for relationship advice, if possible, seek it from those who themselves have happy relationships—this is evidence that they themselves have the "pattern for success" and are more likely to be able to help you!

Chapter summary

- It is easy when you are annoyed to focus on the negatives in your partner.
- Try to "catch yourself" doing this and refocus instead on their positive attributes.
- Focusing on negatives can spill out into criticism.
- Your partner is likely to respond with defensiveness.
- Before you know it, your relationship can become overrun with hostility.
- What you focus on is what you get, so try and focus on the positives in your partner and on showing appreciation for those things. This is

more likely to lead to the supportive relationship that you want.

Chapter 5

How to Communicate Better

"The past is a foreign country; they do things differently there."

— L.P. Hartley, The Go-Between

A couple in a first couples counselling session were very quiet, and reluctant to talk, so I told them a few of the things the research had uncovered about relationships.

The man then said to me "How did you know? —You have just described exactly what is happening with us!"

I replied, "Because it is happening to everybody."

Can I ask you a personal question? Why did you get involved with someone you can't talk to?

I don't mean to be rude, but what sort of numpty starts a relationship with someone with whom they can't communicate?

Not you, I'm sure?

But, maybe you're not so sure, because you can't talk to your partner now, despite your best efforts?

Maybe you haven't been able to talk to them for a very long time.

However, I'm sure that if you search the dark recesses of your mind, you can remember the days after you first met, and I think you'll find that things were very different then.

Can you remember a time when talking to your partner was easy? A joy even? A time when you had fun laughing and chatting together?

Why is it we can all communicate so well in the early days?

I bet you can remember a time, just after you'd first met, when you got on great, when this boy (or girl) seemed like the partner of your dreams?

It's hard to remember since things are so different now but make the effort to stretch your mind back.

I'm sure you'll find that your partner seemed different then: easier to talk to; laid-back even; very different altogether from how they are now? Altogether different from the critical, nagging, clinging, or aggressive nightmare that you seem to be shacked-up with now?

So, what happened?

Was it all a trick? Did they pretend to be different from how they really are? Did they entrap you on purpose by pretending to be so reasonable at the start?

So, I'll ask you that question again: What sort of numpty starts a relationship with someone with whom they can't communicate?

The answer to that question is: no one. No one in their right mind does this.

We fall in love with a person with whom we can communicate well! We all get on well with our partner in the early days.

The problem is that for many people, this changes over time.

But why?

What happens?

The myth of communication

The most common myth about relationships is that good communication is the reason for relationships that work.

Now, don't get me wrong; good communication is important. But it's not the cause of a relationship that works; that is getting cause and effect mixed up.

Problems with communication are not the cause of a difficult relationship. Problems with communication are a symptom of a relationship that is already in difficulty.

The common-sense understanding that communication is important in relationships, is true; but the form that communication needs to take, is primarily listening to your partner.

This is sometimes misunderstood to mean listening to your partner talk about their problems and concerns. But it is important to listen to them talk about everything and nothing! For instance, listen to the things that they are interested in and excited about, even if it is just something they saw on the telly!

When you listen to your partner regularly over weeks, months, and years, it leads to a good, in-depth understanding of what is important to your partner, what they enjoy doing, what they dislike, and what they value in life.

Happily, a good, in-depth understanding of your partner and their world has been found to be protective of a relationship[11] and happily this depth of understanding follows naturally on from regularly listening to them share their daily concerns and enthusiasms.

Listening more effectively

One of the most effective ways of making people feel heard and understood is offering them validation. In his book, *I Hear You,* Michael S. Sorensen argues that effective validation has two components it—identifies a specific emotion (what the other person is feeling) and it offers justification, to them, for feeling that emotion.

It in effect says:

I hear you; I hear what you are feeling, and it is perfectly reasonable to feel that way.

Unfortunately, it is very common to unintentionally invalidate others' feelings (in effect being disrespectful to them) by being too quick to offer advice or by, unintentionally, implying that it is foolish or irrational to feel the way that they do.

For example, by saying "You'll be fine" when someone is worried about something. Probably we all make this mistake sometimes—I know I certainly do!

Although this is often well-meant and is intended as reassurance that everything will be alright in the end, for the person on the receiving end, it can seem to dismiss or belittle their feelings and the challenges that they are facing.

They may hear, "You are being silly to feel the way you do". This can feel unsupportive and dismissive but unfortunately this way of responding to people who are concerned about something is probably the most usual way.

Instead, before we offer any other comment it is usually better to pause to acknowledge and validate the person's feelings, reflecting back to them how they are feeling and stating that it is okay and understandable that they feel that way.

For example, "I'm sorry to hear that you are having such a hard time. It does sound very stressful and difficult and I'm not surprised you are (angry, upset or whatever emotion they have expressed)".

This makes the person feel heard and respected and calms them down, making them more likely to listen to anything else you have to say. This way of responding is sometimes called reflective or active listening (a term first coined by Carl Rodgers) and can be helpful in many situations.

A positive spiral effect

When a relationship is working well, it is easy to communicate well.

In the early days of a relationship, both partners have positive expectations and experiences of the relationship, and as a result, couples communicate well.

Their positive expectations of each other create a spiral effect where they are relaxed and happy talking to each other.

Each of them is enjoying the full attention of the other. They feel attractive and find their new partner attractive.

They lavish affection on each other.

Both feel confident that the other person will listen and engage with them positively.

This is how all long-term relationships begin.

They get along great!

These experiences continue in successful long-term relationships because they keep on getting the little things right.

This creates a culture of positivity and appreciation that makes both partners feel supported and cared for.

This culture of appreciation is created by the three behaviours that heal: attention, affection, and a focus on the positive. These attributes are present in relationships that work, and they make it easy for partners to see and appreciate the good in each other.

Then, when there is conflict, as there always is at some level in relationships, it quickly fizzles out.

It is as if, even during an argument, each partner, in the back of their mind has a little voice saying, "This person loves me; this person is my best mate, and biggest supporter."

And so, because of this, any attempt to end the conflict however inept, is heard, understood, and grabbed at with both hands. It brings the argument to an end.

By contrast, when there is conflict in a relationship were these supportive behaviours are missing, that reassuring voice in the back of the head is absent. At least one partner, and often both, feels neglected and resentful.

So, when an attempt is made to "repair" the argument, it doesn't work.

The partner at whom the repair attempt is aimed, doesn't hear it or doesn't accept it, and the conflict escalates.

Repair attempts that work are one of the biggest predictors of a relationships long-term success. They stop a conflict from escalating out of control.

According to Gottman, "the success or failure of a couple's repair attempts is one of the primary factors in whether [a] marriage is likely to flourish or flounder." He defines a repair attempt as "any statement or action—silly or otherwise— that prevents negativity from escalating out of control."

What determines whether a repair attempt works?

The quality of a couple's friendship before the conflict.

What determines that?—the three behaviours that heal.

When repair attempts fail, conflict escalates, and a relationship starts to become difficult. At this point one partner will often search the internet or the library looking to answer the question, "What can I do? What action can I take to make this situation better?"

Unfortunately, the most likely advice that they will receive, is that they need to communicate better with their partner.

This advice seems good and is understandable, but for reasons that I am going to explain, it leads to a focus on the problem that often makes the situation worse.

Chapter summary

- No one has problems with communication at the start of a long relationship.
- Problems with communication develop later. They are a symptom of a relationship in distress.
- Communication can often be improved by the three behaviours that heal—attention (listening), affection & focusing on the positive.
- These behaviours reduce the tension and hostility in a relationship and so make communicating easier.
- They also improve the quality of the friendship—meaning that repair attempts work, and conflicts don't escalate.
- Validation is often the most helpful, supportive way of responding as a listener—it comprises acknowledging both the other person's feelings and that it is understandable that the person feels that way.

Step Two

Focus on the Solution

Chapter 6

Common Problems in Communication

—how focusing on the problem can make things worse

When a relationship starts to experience difficulty, one partner will often search the internet or the library looking to answer the question, “What can I do? What action can I take to make this situation better?”

Unfortunately, the most likely advice that they will receive, is that they need to communicate better with their partner.

This advice is understandable, but for reasons that I am going to explain, it leads to a focus on the problem which often makes the situation worse.

There are two reasons for this:

1) A problem-focused approach increases the emotional arousal—making it more difficult for everyone to see the big picture and get a perspective on what they are trying to achieve—a loving supportive relationship and a culture of appreciation;

2) Also, there are two very different patterns of physiological response to difficult conversations and this leads to many common problems and misunderstandings in relationships.

The two different patterns of physiological response

One pattern is typically male (in 85 percent of heterosexual marriages one pattern is the husband).[12] The other pattern is typically female.

See if you can guess which one is which. No prizes here, because I bet you can!

The first pattern is that the person feels as though they are under attack the moment a difficult conversation begins.

Their heart rate goes through the roof. They quickly become so physiologically distressed that they are in danger of having a heart-attack.

They typically manage this by either walking out of the discussion or leaving in their mind—that is, zoning out of the situation and trying to calm themselves down with soothing self-talk.

This is often experienced by the other person as talking to a wall, and so is called stonewalling.

Unfortunately, this is very often misinterpreted by the other partner, as being done intentionally to annoy them, or as a sign of immaturity.

It is neither of these things—it is merely a coping mechanism; a way of managing extreme physiological distress.

This common physiological pattern is thought to have evolved from the "hunter/protector" role in early tribal societies and means that some people (mainly men and boys) react very quickly and strongly to any perceived threat and stay in a heightened state of alert for a very long time.

It is thought to be an evolutionary adaptation and is essentially a survival response.

Other people (mainly women and girls) have a very different pattern.

They usually do not respond with a greatly increased heart rate to talking about difficulties in a relationship. If their heart rate does eventually rise, it also returns to its usual rate much quicker than for people with the highly reactive pattern.

Another possible explanation, for this finding is that all people can display this pattern, it is known as the Fight or Flight Response, and is an emergency, survival response.

The real question is why some people (mainly men and boys) react to a difficult conversation as if it were a survival threat and other people (mainly women and girls) do not?

The answer to this may be found in the work of linguist professor Deborah Tannen, who in her book, *You Just Don't Understand*,[13] argues that a different pattern and culture of social interaction and communication is evident between boys and girls from very early childhood.

She argues that boy peer groups compete for and place the highest value on status relative to others whist their female peers, in contrast, place the greatest value on connection.

She suggests that because of this, some men feel that listening at length "frames them as subordinate."

I think it may be that this, combined with our culture's current insistence that the solution to difficulties in a relationship is "better communication" (leading, usually the woman, to insist on talking about difficulties at length), that may explain the extreme stress response found in some men, from the onset of a difficult conversation with their female partner.

Related to this is the common understanding that men and boys are more likely to talk openly when taking part in a group activity or shoulder to shoulder—such as when driving or walking, in contrast to women and girls, who are often comfortable talking about even difficult things, face to face.

From this it follows that some couples might be better having difficult conversations whilst shoulder to shoulder, doing something else, such as gardening or walking.

The problem with focusing on the problem

Whatever the cause, one partner in a typical couple will have one physiological pattern and the other partner will have the other pattern.

The partner that has the highly-reactive, stress-response pattern to difficult conversations, finds that every time their partner starts to talk about an area of conflict, they become extremely physiologically distressed—so distressed that they are in danger of having a heart attack.

And they can stay in this state of physiological distress for a very long time.

People with this pattern feel under attack and find it very difficult to calm themselves down, but they need to calm themselves down because this state is dangerous for them.

They urgently need to remove themselves from this danger and so, what they commonly do, is one of two things:

1) They walk out;

2) They pretend to be somewhere else and, in their mind, try and calm themselves down.

So, completely understandably, after a few of these experiences, this person will then avoid getting into these conversations with their partner—which may be very difficult for them to do, if their partner has read that talking about this stuff helps and is determined to do so!

So, for example, a man that I worked with described how he would sit in silence for up to three hours at a time, whilst his wife talked about their problems. This resulted in him, increasingly avoiding all contact with her.

So, a pattern can quickly develop where one partner starts spending more time in the pub, in the office, or with friends, to avoid the extreme physiological distress, caused by these conversations.

As we have seen, a large contributing factor to relationship difficulties is often lack of attention, so this avoidance of spending time with their partner is highly likely to make things worse.

Therefore, an attempt to solve the problem by talking about the problem often exacerbates the situation, making the difficulties in the relationship worse.

If this is you and this is the pattern you are in - conversations like this, unfortunately, just drive your partner away.

The longer these conversations are and the more often they happen—unfortunately the more likely it is that they will lead to your partner increasingly avoiding spending time with you—which is disastrous for the relationship.

So, what can you do instead?

Action points

1. Focus on the solution.
2. What did you enjoy doing together in the early days? Do more of that! (Get a babysitter if necessary.) The aim is to enable you to start spending time together again in a relaxed, enjoyable way—without talking about problems.
3. Try "walk and talk". Many people who find face-to-face conversations stressful find shoulder to shoulder conversations less so.
4. If you have had lots of long stressful conversations, you might now be almost "allergic" to them. There is an effective technique called The Rewind Technique that can help to break these unhelpful associations and so reduce the stress they trigger. You can find an international register of qualified practitioners here: https://www.hgi.org.uk/find-therapist
5. Rehearse success (see Chapter 10).
6. Eventually, when the tension between you has reduced (a lot!), you can learn how to talk about your difficulties in a different way: in a way that your partner can hear you (see Chapter 9, How to Complain).

Chapter summary

- A problem-focused approach increases the emotional arousal—making it more difficult for everyone to see the big picture and get a perspective on what they are trying to achieve.
- There are two common patterns of physiological reactivity during a difficult conversation.
- One pattern is to become extremely physiologically distressed very rapidly. Most people who have this pattern are male. It is thought to be an evolutionary adaptation and is essentially a survival response— so it is not in their control.
- The other pattern is to have a much longer, slower build up to becoming physiologically distressed and a much faster recovery.
- The pattern of extreme physiological distress commonly results in people walking out of difficult discussions or stonewalling.
- Stonewalling is when someone mentally blocks out a difficult conversation in order to calm down. It can feel to the other person like talking to a wall.

- It is an attempt to calm themselves down but is often misunderstood.
- Because of this, trying to solve a problem in the relationship by talking about it repeatedly or at length can, in some couples, lead to one partner increasingly avoiding the other.
- It is not that you shouldn't try and address problems in your relationship—of course you should—it's just important how you go about doing that (see Action points above).

Step Three

Support Your Partner to Get their Needs Met

Chapter 7

Emotional Needs and Resources

A relationship doesn't happen in a vacuum, so when things are going wrong, you also need to have a good look at what else is happening around you.

How balanced is your own life? How balanced is your partner's life? What other things are impacting on your relationship? What essential needs are being met or not being met for you both? What are your stressors? Are they permanent or temporary? What can you do to alleviate them?

Everyone knows that, as human beings, we all have physical needs, for example for water, food, and oxygen. What is less well-known, is that we also have emotional needs, such as a need for safety and security, emotional connection, meaning, and belonging.

When our emotional needs are not sufficiently met, we can become emotionally ill, with stress, anxiety, or depression. If our emotional needs are met well, particularly if each need is met through multiple sources, we will be more resilient to life's many stressors and challenges.

In a relationship, obviously both people's needs are important. If someone is very unhappy, stressed or anxious, it is very likely that at least one of their essential needs is not being met. When that is the case, it can often impact on the relationship—and sometimes they can think that it is the relationship that is at fault, when in reality it is that their life is out of balance and important needs are not being met.

Some people feel that all their emotional needs must be met by their partner; because of this, they can become over-dependent on their partner.

Dependence makes us unhealthily reliant on one person. If that relationship breaks down or the other person becomes seriously ill or incapacitated, we are on our own. One partner being over-dependent on the other, can put both partners under a lot of strain. To get our needs met in balance, we probably need to be inter-dependent.

Independence is where we are self-reliant and stand on our own feet.

Dependence is when we get most or all of our needs met through one other person. This is sometimes called co-dependence when two people are over- reliant on one another.

Inter-dependence is increasingly seen as the healthiest model. Inter-dependence is when we are self-reliant but meet our needs through a range of relationships and activities (such as friends, family, neighbours and colleagues).

Inter-dependence leaves us more resilient in the face of adversity. It gives us multiple sources of the things that we need.

Our Essential Emotional Needs[14] are:

Safety—Freedom from experiencing real or imagined danger.

Security—The ability to plan and feel confident about important aspects of our lives, such as our finances, our employment, our living arrangements, and our relationships.

Belonging to a wider community—This may be, for instance, a community of neighbours, friends, a social or sports club, members of a religious or spiritual community, or a political group.

Privacy—Time on our own to reflect on our lives and consolidate new learning, and to deal, without embarrassment, with our bodily functions.

Emotional connection—A sense of being known and understood by at least one other person. Knowing that someone is there for us and that we can be completely ourselves with them.

Control—The ability to make decisions about at least some aspects of our lives.

Giving and receiving attention—Feeling that we are giving & receiving enough attention.

Swapping attention with healthy individuals helps to keep us sane. It allows us to check our own model of reality against other people's models. It stops us from losing our moorings and helps keep us grounded.

However, it is essential that the people we swap attention with regularly, are reasonably healthy, otherwise we may just reinforce a view of reality that is distorted.

For example, people who tend to get depressed need to be careful not to spend too much time with others who are depressed because of the danger of themselves taking on an unhealthily pessimistic and negative view of the world.

Meaning and purpose—Our need for meaning can be met in many ways by contributing positively to our families, our communities, and the wider world and by living in congruence with our deepest values.

Status—Most of us need to feel valued by those around us. If we are a cleaner for example, it is possible for us to have this need met through our work, if everyone around us understands and values our contribution.

Even if we are the CEO, it is also possible for us not to have this need met, if the people around us belittle us and undermine us and make us feel that our contribution is not valued.

Real life examples

If someone is at risk of losing their job, and is unsure about finding another one, this can impact on their needs for security, control, and status.

They may start worrying about their situation and whether they will be able to pay the mortgage or rent, and whether they will lose their home.

It is this impact on essential emotional needs that can make some situations lead to worsening emotional health: stress, anxiety, and sometimes depression.

Many of our emotional needs have to do with our relationships with other people. Being unable to get along easily with other people because of a lack of social skills or because of bad experiences can impact on our emotional health.

If someone has poor social skills, maybe because they are shy and self-conscious, or because they have not had the opportunity to learn them, or because they have had difficult experiences, this can have an impact on their ability to get their emotional needs met.

In some cases, it can result in a cascade of difficult experiences, which can ultimately lead to serious emotional health problems.

Needs that may not be met due to a lack of social skills include emotional connection, giving and receiving attention, status, belonging, safety and security.

Your need vs my need

Ongoing arguments can be solvable or unsolvable. Many couples have unsolvable disagreements because their needs and wants or the "dreams" they represent are in conflict. This doesn't necessarily mean that the relationship will break up.

There is no solution for this other than good will, to keep talking, and a recognition that both partners are just trying to get important needs met.

For example, one couple I worked with each had a very different dream, though they both wanted eventually to have a family and they were planning to buy a house together.

He wanted to be close to his parents, his friends and his work in the city centre. He ideally wanted to live on an estate, a close commute from the city, and near all modern conveniences.

She ideally wanted an outdoor, eco-friendly lifestyle. Her dream was to eventually build a smallholding business growing organic vegetables and flowers and to raise animals such as goats, sheep and chickens.

They had compromised on the idea of buying a house with a large garden that was close to his work and to modern conveniences but were arguing a lot.

In order to retain her dream, she wanted to "rewild" the garden and keep chickens. This was a red line for her, but he and his friends and family thought it completely unreasonable.

They didn't see or understand her dream or how far she had already come to meet him halfway. They were close to splitting up about this and every house they saw led to yet another argument about the garden and what it would be used for.

During our work together I helped them to uncover and see their competing "dreams" which they had not previously been fully aware of. Once they understood each other better they were eventually able to find a different compromise that worked better for them both.

Our Resources

As with all living things, we are born with innate resources[15] that can help us to get our needs met.

Our innate needs and resources together make up the Human Givens. These are bedrock truths about what human beings need to thrive, which have been established by research over the last fifty years.

When we are stressed, anxious, or depressed, doing an audit of our emotional needs can help us to better understand what is going on and where to focus our efforts. You can find a link to an Emotional Needs Audit at the back of this book in Further Reading and Resources.

Our innate resources include:

- The ability to develop complex long-term memory which enables us to add to our knowledge and learn;
- The ability to understand the world instinctively through metaphorical pattern-matching;
- The ability to build rapport, empathise and connect with others;
- Imagination, which enables us to focus our attention away from our emotions and problem solve more creatively and objectively by seeing patterns and "the big picture";
- A conscious, rational mind that can create strategies, plans, and solutions—and works

best when we are calm and focused 100% on the task in hand;

- A dreaming brain that preserves the integrity of our genetic inheritance every night by metaphorically defusing emotionally arousing expectations not acted out the previous day;
- An observing self that can stand back and observe our thoughts, actions, and experiences, and reflect on them.

Other resources that we may also have, that can help us:

- Life experiences—good and bad
- Successes
- Failures—and what you've learnt from them
- Achievements
- Challenges and difficulties, we've overcome
- Coping skills
- Social skills
- Knowledge
- Qualifications

- Work experience—including voluntary work experience
- Friends
- Neighbours
- Family
- Community—such as, social clubs, churches, charities, schools and sport clubs
- Talents
- Interests
- Hobbies
- Things you enjoy
- Things you love

Chapter summary

- Relationships don't happen in a vacuum—we need to look after ourselves and each other.
- As living creatures, we have physical needs and we are all aware that, when they go unmet, we can become physically ill.

- But humans also have emotional needs. We tend to be less aware of these needs, and the fact that we can become emotionally ill if they are not met sufficiently.

- Like all living creatures, we are born with innate resources that can help us ensure that our needs are met.

- When one of us is stressed, anxious, or depressed, doing an audit of our emotional needs can help us better understand what is going on.

- Our innate needs and resources together, make up the Human Givens which are bedrock truths about what human beings really need to thrive.

Chapter 8

Romance and Intimacy

A Word About Sex

This is an area in which many couples experience difficulties, so I will include lots of links to further information and other resources in the back of this book, but I also want to make a few broad points (some of which apply mainly to heterosexual couples).

For most women and some men, the desire to have sex in a relationship is, in my experience, completely dependent on how they feel about their partner in general.

In other words, making your partner feel loved, cared for, and supported, goes a long way towards sorting out any difficulties in this area.[16]

This is particularly so when the difficulty is that a partner who was once enthusiastic about sex, now appears to have lost all interest in it.

If your partner is feeling resentful towards you because you're not listening when they want to talk to you about things that are important to them (but may not be important to you), they are not going to look kindly at overtures towards sex later that day, or anytime soon.

In unhappy relationships, at least one partner—often both—is feeling completely unloved, neglected and, because of this, resentful.

Ultimately, their needs in the relationship are not met. For a relationship to work long-term, both partners need to have their needs met in a balanced way.

If your partner has been feeling neglected, unloved, and resentful for years—as many partners in unhappy relationships have—the relationship will be close to breakdown.

In this scenario, it is unlikely that you will still be enjoying regular sex together.

Indeed, in this situation, it is more likely that sex has become just another chore, another demand, for at least one partner and often, this has been the case for years.

Often, one partner—usually, but not always, the woman—will complain about a lack of emotional connection and romance.

Of course, romance can mean many different things to different people. One useful question to ask yourself is, “What did my partner enjoy in the past?”

Sometimes, in this situation, affection will feel difficult. To the partner who is feeling unloved and neglected, a gesture of affection may be suspected to be just a tool being used as a lead-in to sex.

This can make a partner feel used and even more resentful.

Romantic gestures such as flowers or a candlelit meal can also be devalued in this way, however good the intention. If it feels to one partner that these things are only ever part of a request for sex, they will lose interest.

This is unfortunately common and ultimately counterproductive as it increases bad feelings and distrust.

If you are the partner who is always hoping for more sexual intimacy, try to be affectionate at other times without it always having to be about sex.

In these circumstances, it can be helpful to break the pattern by refraining from attempts to initiate sex – say for a month or six weeks – and to instead focus on bringing back the romance (see Case Study 2).

You may also find the book, *The 5 Love Languages* (see Further Reading) helpful with this. In this book, the therapist Gary Chapman explores in detail ways to express love and affection, so that your partner can feel it.

Also, remember the other two behaviours that heal and make them part of your daily life:

1) Attention and
2) Focus on the positive

I've seen many people who have done this.

After many weeks of feeling that they were getting nowhere they suddenly report that they have turned the corner and are back on track; back to cuddling, sleeping together, having days out with the kids, and having fun together in all its forms.

Often, all it takes is for at least one of you to "keep on keeping on"—as the song has it—because what goes wrong between people is a dynamic. If one person changes, the whole relationship can change.

However, be warned that you will need perseverance and determination to keep this up—day after day, week after week—often with nothing to show for it for a long time. So, think of it as a marathon rather than a sprint!

It can also be helpful to think of it as "winning your partner back"—a period of courtship to show them how much you love and value them (remember they are probably feeling neglected and hurt).

More problems with sex

Women were traditionally the gatekeepers for sex, as before reliable DNA tests, the only guarantee of paternity was the faithfulness of the woman.

In many cultures and time periods, women have been under huge pressure to be or appear to be asexual and chaste.

Even today, there are still very mixed messages in society about women's sexuality. In many cultures, sexuality and enjoyment of sex is seen as a good thing—in men and boys.

By contrast, virginity and chastity are still prized and even venerated, in women, in many religions and cultures. As a result, many people grew up believing that sex is something for men that is done to women.

There are still many insults available to shame women—but not men—who are sexually active. All these mixed, conflicting messages—not surprisingly—cause some women (and some men) problems in this area.

Women and girls often feel that they are expected to be sexy, but not sexual.[18]

In addition, whereas the most sexual part of a man's body (the penis) is clearly visible to them, and they are familiar with it and used to handling it from a young age, the most sexual part of a woman's body (the clitoris) is not necessarily familiar to her.

Also, because it has no function in reproduction (other than the pleasure of the woman) its importance has been overlooked in many cultures, until recently.

What women like sexually is not normally what we see in depictions of sex. Even today, male pleasure remains centre stage.

Clitoral stimulation, which is central to most female's pleasure, still isn't usually shown in sex on screen, however otherwise explicit. It is also often not part of sex education despite its crucial role in sex for half the population.

Sex therapists say that enjoyment of sex is first learnt through masturbation, but this is something that, for all these reasons, many women didn't do and don't feel comfortable with.

Because of all this, a woman may not have learnt to enjoy her own body and may not be in touch with her own sexuality. These difficulties can be passed down from mother to daughter as well as through the wider culture; for example, through attitudes towards masturbation.

Like men, women must be aroused to enjoy sex. However, for all the reasons given above, many women have had even consensual sex, particularly when young, where they were not sufficiently aroused, and it was painful and unpleasant.

All of this, sadly, means that although women, in my experience, are as capable of enjoying sex as men, many women and girls have had only bad or frustrating experiences.

Times are changing—and thankfully, this is not the case for increasing numbers of women—but cultural practices and attitudes change slowly, so these things still affect many women and relationships today.

The effects of trauma

Another area of possible difficulty for both men and women is the effects of trauma. Experiences of sexual abuse and rape are unfortunately not uncommon and can leave survivors with long-lasting difficulties in many areas, often, especially in sexual relationships.

Human Givens Therapy has a specific evidence-based, intervention for trauma and other difficult experiences, which is very effective, in many cases, in relieving symptoms and distress. It does not involve re-living or talking in detail about what happened.

You can find more information about this method here:

http://www.ptsdresolution.org/key-facts.php

An international register of therapists fully trained in this therapy can be found at

https://www.hgi.org.uk/

Chapter summary

- Many couples experience difficulties in this area.
- If your partner is feeling resentful towards you, they are unlikely to look kindly at overtures towards sex later that day, or anytime soon.
- If you are hoping for more sexual intimacy, try to be affectionate at other times without it always having to be about sex.
- In these circumstances, it can be helpful to break the pattern by refraining from attempts to initiate sex—say for a month or six weeks—and to instead focus on bringing back the romance.

Step Four

Complain, don't Criticise

Chapter 9

How to Complain

So, the first thing to note about this is that there is no point in being great at communicating if your partner won't listen, and if they don't feel loved and supported, then they're not going to give you a fair hearing—no matter how great you are communicating.

Presuming then, that you're making efforts to help your partner feel loved and supported, as explained in the previous chapters, the next thing to do is to start as you mean to go on—gently.

The research is clear that in difficult conversations "the start predicts the end".

In other words, if you start harshly, it increases the chances that the conversation will end badly.

So, what you want to aim at, is to start gently.

Research has found that people who are great at relationships, “The Masters”, start a difficult conversation gently.[18]

Of course, most of us aren’t masters, we are more like disasters!

When we want to complain, many of us make the mistake of criticising instead. This, unfortunately, makes it harder for our partners to hear us, because it makes them feel attacked.

We say things like, “You do this”, and “You do that”, and “People like you...” This makes the other person feel blamed and criticised. It feels to them as though we are pointing an accusing finger at them.

What the masters do instead, is use “I” statements, instead of “you” statements.

They talk about themselves and their own emotions, and when they complain, they complain about only one thing at a time. This makes it easier for the other person to hear.

So, for instance, they might say: "I am scared when I look at our bank balance. I need us to find ways of managing our money better." Or, they might say,

"I was upset, when I came down this morning because the kitchen was a mess. I would really like us all to find ways of keeping the kitchen tidier in the evenings."

Or;

"I was upset when I came down this morning because there were wet towels on the bathroom floor. I wish you could hang up the towels after you shower."

Notice that they always start with an "I" statement and follow that with an emotion.

Any emotion will do: I am sad, I am hurt, I am angry, I am upset. "I am upset" is a good one, because it is very general—it can cover a lot.

The research is clear that starting a difficult conversation gently, predicts it ending well.

Notice also that the masters are very specific in what they're complaining about.

Lots of us tend to "throw in the kitchen sink" when we're complaining. We bring up everything!

Unfortunately, this makes the other person feel attacked, and less likely to listen to us.

Remember:

What we are aiming for is to complain, not to criticise.

Complaints are concrete, specific, and limited to one thing.

Criticism is more general and personal.

For example, a complaint might be:

"I am upset that I always have to take the bins out. I would like us to take turns."

Notice the structure of the sentence:

"I" statement, followed by

Emotion, e.g. "am upset," followed by

Specific complaint, e.g. "that I always have to take the bins out."

Followed by being specific about what they would like instead: "I would like us to take turns."

Criticism (about the same thing) might look like:

"You are so lazy! Why do you never take the bins out? I am fed up—I do everything around here!"

Notice:

1. "You" followed by,
2. Insult— "...are so lazy!" followed by,
3. Other issues— "I do everything around here!"

A complaint is easier for your partner to hear than criticism, which is more personal and all-encompassing.

Of course, if you do fall into the trap of making more than one complaint at a time, this will feel like criticism to your partner. Try to stick to one thing if your aim is to complain.

Even if you do get this right, if your partner has often felt criticised in the past, they may mistake a complaint for criticism.

In that case, state as soon as possible, "I am not intending to criticise you. I just want to let you know how this (one specific thing) makes me feel."

Another thing to bear in mind, for difficult conversations, is that it is important to get your timing right.

Think about when the best time would be to have this conversation. Ideally, a time when you are both relaxed and getting along well—so, not when your partner is stressed, tired and has just come in from work!

Something else to bear in mind is your tone of voice and your body language. Try to avoid starting an important conversation when you are very emotional.

We communicate more through our tone of voice and our body language, than through our words.

A simple way to get this right, is to spend some time getting into a positive frame of mind about your partner before you start this conversation. Think about the things you like about your partner, what first attracted you to him or her, and about the good qualities they have.

If you find this difficult, remind yourself of your own faults—none of us is perfect!

Also, remind yourself that all personal traits have two sides: a good side and a bad. For example, someone who is very tidy and clean may be easier to live with in some ways than someone who is messy.

However, the neat and tidy person may find it hard to relax when things are not tidy and may apply their own exacting standards to everyone else, which can also be stressful to live with.

Someone who is very relaxed and easy-going, by contrast, may not be so good at keeping things tidy and clean, but might be easier to live with in other ways. For instance, they may not sweat the small stuff!

Another thing you can do to prepare for a difficult conversation, is to use positive visualization to rehearse success. I explain what this is and how you can use it to help you in the next chapter.

Chapter summary

- How a conversation begins predicts how it will end—so start gently.
- Use "I" statements—not "You" statements—followed by an emotion.
- Stick to one specific issue.
- Ask for what you need. For example, "I need us to find ways of managing our money better."
- If your partner becomes defensive, say, "I am not intending to criticise you. I just want you

to understand how this (one thing) made me feel."

Step Five

Use your Brain

Chapter 10

Rehearsing Success

"Imagination is more important than knowledge"

—Albert Einstein

We can know that these things make sense and yet, still have difficulty making the changes we know that we need to make to our daily behaviour. This is where relaxation combined with positive visualization can help.

Our brains follow patterns. Our imagination can help us to lay down healthy patterns for our brains to follow. It can help us to translate our goals and intentions into concrete changes to our behaviour.

Positive visualization is currently most often used by sports psychologists to coach athletes to perform better. However, it has wide applicability and is something we can all use to help us in everyday life.

It can help us to use patterns of success, and how our brains work best, to help us handle difficult situations and conversations well.

When we are stressed, the thinking parts of our brain shut down and we become trapped in our emotions.[19] This is what people mean when they say, "I can't think straight." Whereas when we are calm, we have access to our whole brain.

We can perform at our best in any situation when we are:

1) calm, and

2) 100% focused on the task in hand.

People who perform badly often have a split focus, in that only fifty percent of their attention is on the task in hand.

The other fifty percent of their attention is on themselves and worrying about how they are coming across to other people—whether they are stuttering, blushing, or making a fool of themselves in some way.

When we are anxious and stressed about something, we are likely to focus on how things could go wrong. Our brains follow patterns, so this unfortunately, means that we are in fact rehearsing failure.

This is a misuse of our imagination, a sure way for our efforts to be in vain.

Positive visualization allows us instead, to use our imagination well, to help us overcome our difficulties.

Using our brain as our own reality simulator to practise patterns of success and foresee any potential difficulties increases our chances of handling a difficult conversation or situation well.

People who do something well are often already doing this.

I once read an interview with a successful athlete and he commented that he had found psychological coaching of no benefit at all. However, it was clear to me from the other things he said that this was because he was using all their methods already!

A good example is of the benefits of positive visualization to someone preparing for an interview.

If they have had bad past experiences during interviews, they will think about all the things that could go wrong.

This will increase their anxiety about the interview and mean that the stress hormone, cortisol, will flood their brain, affecting their ability to think clearly. Here is how that works:

Pattern for failure

Lucy hates interviews. She's always been bad at them. She's anxious because of all her past bad experiences.

As she prepares, she thinks of all the things that have gone wrong in the past and all the things that could go wrong now.

This makes her feel stressed and anxious, so her thinking brain shuts down. As a result of this, she finds it hard to think clearly and has difficulty preparing herself properly.

In the lead-up to the interview, she sees herself doing badly. She sees herself becoming embarrassed, blushing, and stammering.

She has difficulties focusing properly on her preparations for the interview, which only increases her anxiety. On the day of the interview, she continues to see herself doing badly, in her mind's eye.

She is anxious and stressed going into the interview, so only half of her attention is on the task in hand, the other half of her attention is on herself; she worries that she is blushing and stammering and about what the interviewers will think of her.

This anxiety traps her in her emotions, making it difficult for her to focus properly on what she is being asked and to answer as well as she can.

Pattern for success

Helen loves interviews. She's always been good at them and enjoyed them.

When she prepares for an interview, she is calm and relaxed and focused on the task at hand. In the lead-up to the interview she sees herself doing well— listening carefully to the questions and answering calmly and clearly.

Because she is calm her brain works at its best, so she can prepare herself well.

On the day of the interview, she again sees herself in her mind's-eye doing well.

So, when she walks in, she is calm, confident and focused 100% outwards on answering the questions and presenting herself, as well as she can. Because she is calm, her brain works well; the words come easily, and she can perform at her best.

Notice that she can only control her own behaviour and attitudes. The outcome of the interview is not in her control, no matter what she does!

How to rehearse a difficult conversation

To make a difficult conversation more likely to go well, we can prepare ourselves well and use positive visualization to help us translate our good intentions into real life behaviour. It is important to be relaxed when you do this rehearsal of success, so that you can access the appropriate parts of the brain.

This is what to do:

1) Choose a time and place where you are safe to sit or lie down comfortably and switch off; some place where you can relax. The time just before you go to sleep is good, or just before you get up in the morning. If you are

relaxed already you can go straight on to step 8.

2) Make sure you are comfortable. Focus on your body and ensure you're not holding tension in your shoulders or anywhere else in your body. Check that your arms, your hands, your legs, and your feet are relaxed.

3) Ensure that your forehead is smooth, and your tongue is loose in your jaw. Spread feelings of comfort and relaxation throughout all parts of your body.

4) Focus on your breathing—the gentle rise and fall of your chest that happens all by itself. Increase your out-breath. Make it nice and long—longer than your in-breath.

5) In your mind's eye, go to somewhere beautiful in nature; some place where you can relax and enjoy the peace and beauty around you. Maybe you would like to go for a gentle stroll?

6) Notice what you can see around you—in the distance and what you can see closer to you. Notice the colours around you and the patterns the light is making.

7) Notice the sensation of the breeze or the sun on your skin. Notice the sky. Are there fluffy, white clouds and a gentle breeze or is

it a beautiful, sunny day and you can feel the sun warm on your skin?

8) Now that you're comfortable and relaxed, imagine yourself preparing the conversation or the situation that you want to rehearse. Imagine that you are calm in the lead-up to this situation.

9) You are preparing yourself calmly and because of this, you have access to all your brain, your intelligence, your experience, your strengths, your resources, and you are focused outwards on preparing well for the task at hand.

10) Imagine yourself, in the lead-up to this conversation, thinking positively about your partner, about the reasons you were attracted to them in the first place, about their strengths, and the things you like about them.

11) Imagine that as you go into the situation or conversation, you are relaxed and calm and 100% focused outwards on the task at hand—on behaving as you would like to behave, and on managing the situation well.

12) Imagine choosing your time well and starting softly and gently; starting the conversation by using a positive tone of voice and open, non-threatening, body language.

13) See yourself using "I" statements, plus how you feel, for example, "I am hurt," or "I am upset."

14) Imagine yourself sticking to one specific complaint and reassuring your partner by stating that you don't intend to criticise them; you just want to explain how you feel about this one particular thing.

15) Imagine that however the conversation goes you remain calm and focused on behaving well.

16) When you get up, have a stretch and maybe a glass of water.

WARNING: Ensure that you are fully alert before driving or operating machinery.

Anything that makes you relax, for instance, some types of yoga, can potentially, help you open up your thinking brain, access your resources and your imagination, and provide an opportunity for you to rehearse success in any challenges you are facing.

It is important that when you are in that relaxed state, you focus on the positives and on the outcomes that you want.

Use these times to remind yourself of your skills, your values, your achievements, and your strengths.

Remind yourself of those things when you are facing challenging times, because we all need to do that.

Remember, you can't control what your partner or anybody else does. You can only determine your own attitudes and behaviours. Focus on these!

Chapter summary

- Our brains follow patterns and positive visualization can help us to lay down healthy patterns for our brains to follow.
- It can help us translate our goals and intentions into concrete changes to our behaviour by using our mind to rehearse success.
- When we are stressed the thinking parts of our brain shut down and we become trapped in our emotions. This is what people mean when they say, "I can't think straight."
- Relaxation opens our thinking brain, allowing us to better access our imagination and providing an opportunity for us to rehearse success in any challenges we are facing.

Chapter 11

The Importance of Calm

In highly emotional situations, it helps to step away—get perspective, see what's really important and what we are in danger of losing.

In long-term relationships we need to look after ourselves and each other. To do this, we need to understand what it is that we each need to thrive.

In any situation, we can only work on ourselves—our piece of the jigsaw, no matter how much we may feel that it is all our partners fault!

One thing that is commonly underestimated is the importance of relaxation and calm in our lives. People think that they should always be doing something and busy rushing around.

Time relaxing is often seen as wasted time and people even feel guilty for spending time doing nothing. With the pressure of modern times, this is how many of us live; however, it is not good for us.

As human beings, we essentially have two modes of operation. One is the relaxation mode— sometimes called "rest and digest" and the other is the "fight or flight" survival mode. We function best when we have balance in our lives and have both periods of being busy and active and also regular periods of relaxation.

Unfortunately, many people today are spending most of their time in the fight or flight, survival mode. This is what we describe as being stressed.

There's a lot of confusion today about stress. So, let us look a little bit at what we really mean by being stressed.

Some people say that stress is good for us. This is because they are confusing stress with stretch. Being stretched is good for us but it is different from being stressed.[20]

Every system has a breaking point at which the pressures on it can overwhelm its ability to cope. This is what is really meant by stress.

At its most extreme, stress can lead to an inability to function which is commonly referred to as "burn out" or a "nervous breakdown".

Stress is what happens when the pressures we are facing overwhelm our capabilities and spare capacity.

Being stretched is something different. Being stretched is when we're challenged to move out of our comfort zone and grow. This is healthy.

We are living creatures. If we are not growing, moving, and changing, we often stagnate—like water. Challenge and growth are good for us, so long as they are commensurate with our capabilities.

No one's capabilities are limitless—whatever they tell us or would like us to believe!

When we are stressed, our bodies go into survival mode—preparing us to run or to fight. That is why this is called the fight or flight response.

Our brain thinks that there is an emergency, so our normal bodily maintenance functions—such as digestion—are turned down or off. Instead, all the body's main organs-such as the lungs and the heart prioritise sending oxygen to the muscles in our legs and arms.

The physical changes that occur when we are stressed are all caused by this prioritisation of sending oxygen to our large muscles so that we can fight or run away.

That is why, when we are stressed, our heart beats faster, our breathing speeds up and we hyperventilate. It also explains many of the symptoms that people commonly experience and associate with anxiety and stress.

When we are stressed, our digestion shuts down, because this is an emergency and, in an emergency, digesting food properly is not a priority.

So, for example, our saliva dries up—which we may experience as a dry mouth and we may have pains or funny sensations in our stomach or abdomen, because our digestive processes are shutting down.

This process, as well as affecting our digestion of food also puts a lot of pressure on our hearts.[21] Therefore, being stressed is not good for us.

This part of our response to stress is common knowledge, but there is another part of our response to stress that is much less well-known. It happens at the level of our brain.

Our brain is also affected by stress hormones—particularly by cortisol, during the fight or flight response. This hormone also acts as a neurotransmitter and can close down the neocortex, the higher thinking parts of the brain, reducing our ability to think clearly.

This happens when we are stressed, anxious, or in any way very emotional. The amygdala “hijacks” our neocortex and we become trapped in our emotions.

This affects our ability to think, plan, strategise, and perform well. Over time, chronic stress can also lead to changes in our Hippocampus, an area of the brain with a central role in memory, impairing our memory.[22]

For all these reasons, long periods of stress are best avoided and bringing calm and relaxation into our lives is far from “wasting time”.

An easy, effective method of becoming calm quickly is to focus on lengthening our out-breath. Our out-breath is naturally relaxing. This method of relaxation is called 7/11 breathing.

It is also possible to purchase a recording to help you to relax. I include a link to one in the further reading and resources chapter at the back of this book.

An interesting, related fact is that smokers often say that they find smoking relaxing but, in fact cigarettes don't contain anything that relaxes you.[23]

What they are more likely to be finding relaxing is the breathing pattern of smoking: a short inhalation followed by a very long exhalation. This is 7/11 breathing!

And the good news is—we can all do this, with no cigarette necessary, and we can practise it wherever we are and whenever we like.

It is a useful tool to have. Practise it regularly, so that you remember it, when you need it, in times of stress or anxiety.

Chapter summary

- In high emotion situations, it helps to step away—get perspective, see what's really important and what we are in danger of losing.
- Stress is what happens when the pressures we are facing overwhelm our capabilities.

- It is not healthy as it adversely affects our digestion, puts our heart under pressure, and affects our ability to think and speak clearly.
- Long-term stress can also impair our memory.
- Being stretched is different. This is when we are challenged within our capabilities and it is healthy.
- Time relaxing allows us to digest our food well and fully access the higher parts of our brain, allowing us to think more clearly and potentially to be more effective, creative and productive.
- 7/11 breathing is a simple & effective way of relaxing quickly, whenever and wherever we want to.

Chapter 12

Putting It All Together

My Story: Part 2

The reason why I became interested and immersed myself in this research, is that I was the world's worst at this!

My partner was always trying to get my attention about topics that were important to him but were not necessarily as important to me.

Unfortunately, I had fallen into the very bad habit of reading constantly. My partner would be trying to get my attention, and I would often be going, "Yeah, yeah,

yeah, yeah." I would be completely neglectful and rude in my response.

I was oblivious to the damage that this behaviour was doing to our relationship. My behaviour was giving my partner the message: "I don't love you, I don't care about you, I'm not there for you." Even though this wasn't at all how I felt.

So, very soon after reading the first few chapters of The Relationship Cure, I came to an awful realisation. The foremost authority on relationships in the world was predicting that my own relationship would end, and he was saying that this would happen because of my behaviour. This was horrifying to me!

My behaviour of failing to look up, listen to my partner and respond appropriately when he was talking to me, was predicted to lead to increasing amounts of conflict in the relationship.

These rows would become worse and worse and would eventually lead to the relationship breaking down.

John Gottman, the world's leading authority on relationships, was predicting that our relationship would end.

I was at fault—and I hadn't even realised the enormous damage that my behaviour was doing.

So, when I realised this, I vowed that I would change.

I didn't tell my husband about what I had read. I just decided to change my behaviour.

But it was actually really tough! The reason it was tough is because when you're reading, or watching television, or on your phone, your attention is locked, and it takes enormous effort to unlock it and pay attention to your partner instead.

I had to train myself to look up and say to myself, "Brain to Ann Marie! Your partner is trying to talk to you about something that is important to him. Listen to him!

If you do this, that will show him that you love him, that you care for him, that you are supportive of him. It will demonstrate that more than anything else you can do! Brain to Ann Marie! Put that book down!"

And so, I had to—slowly, painfully—teach myself that when my partner started to talk to me, I should put my book, newspaper, or iPad down and refocus my full attention on listening and trying to understand what he was saying.

I had to constantly remind myself of why this was important and to show him clearly that I was listening.

After this, I found that the rows that we'd started to have, fizzled out more quickly. Over the next few months, the relationship became more affectionate and supportive, and conflict happened less and less.

Now, of course, you can't always stop what you're doing. You can't always give someone your full attention. So sometimes, you do need to say, "I'm sorry. I'm in the middle of something just now, can I get back to you later on this?"

Then, of course, you do need to get back to them later and make the time to listen to them talk about whatever it is they wanted to tell you.

And remember, often the conversations that are most important look like they are about nothing at all.

Everyday conversations about what's on the TV, or about the football, or the dog—are the important conversations; the ones that make all the difference, even though they seem—to most people—to be completely trivial and about absolutely nothing.

So, if you're recognising yourself and your own relationships in what I'm describing, as people often do, what you need to do is to start focusing on changing these little behaviours.

Don't despair if things are going very badly just now. In my experience, if even one partner makes the effort to change these behaviours (even if the other partner won't come for help) surprisingly, even in these cases, I have found that it can be possible to turn things around.

If one partner is prepared to do these three things—provide attention, affection, and focus on the positives—every day, come rain or shine; come praise or criticism, that may be enough to restore relationship harmony over time.

Because a relationship is a dynamic between people, a change in attitude and behaviour by one person is often enough to change the attitude and behaviour of the other person.

It is like an energy that is passed from one person to another.

What I usually find, when at least one partner does this, is that the tensions go down and the expectations of both partners start to improve of each other and of the relationship.

This is because at least one partner is now getting essential emotional needs met through the relationship. Usually, that person at some point starts to reciprocate.

This then leads to both partners feeling much happier with the way things are going.

They start to develop the positive expectations of each other and of the relationship that are found in relationships that work.

Our most important needs in a relationship are for attention and affection. So, when those two needs are met by our partner, we start to feel loved, supported, and cared for, and that can make all the difference.

When brought together with a focus on the positive, this has the potential to "pour oil on the cogs" of the relationship, making everything go more smoothly.

So, when even one partner starts to do this, the other partner very often calms down and starts responding in kind.

The partner on the receiving end, starts to feel loved and appreciated, instead of criticised and unappreciated, and stops feeling the need to be defensive. Instead, they start to feel that their partner is "there" for them.

After all, that is probably what many people want most from a long-term relationship—we want to feel that the other person is “there” for us; in the sense that we can rely on them to support and care for us when it really counts.[24]

And so, when one partner starts to feel like this, very often it has the effect of turning the whole relationship round.

People start naturally to communicate well—because they are getting on better.

Conflict starts to fizzle out because repair attempts are heard.

With time this can create an atmosphere of appreciation and love in the home. If there are children, it is likely to also have a positive, calming effect on the whole family.

However, if it is you who is trying to make these changes, realise that although it is little things that need changing, it can take a lot of effort.

At first, a lot of this will probably feel unnatural.

This can make the advice that I’m giving more difficult to carry out than it seems.

But, like anything else we practise, it will become easier with time.

End Note

Relationships are complicated. No book can hope to cover all scenarios.

If in doubt, the best thing to do is to seek professional help.

These are two international registers of therapists using evidence-based methods:

Find a Therapist

With the Gottman Institute (specialising in relationships)

https://www.gottman.com/couples/private-

With the Human Givens Institute (specialising in a solution-focused approach)

https://www.hgi.org.uk/find-therapist

Chapter summary

- Even if just one partner starts bringing in attention, affection and focusing on the positives, over time it can often turn around a relationship.
- When we are busy doing something, our attention is locked, and it needs a lot of effort to refocus our attention on listening to our partner.
- Keep up the effort—this is all important if you want your love to last!
- At first, this will probably feel unnatural but, like anything else we practise, it will become easier with time.

Case Study One*

Session 1

(*These case studies are based on real cases but all names and other potentially identifying details have been changed.)

John, who is in his late twenties, came to see me. He was a tradesman and had built his own house in which he lived with his girlfriend. They had two young children, a couple of dogs and had been having a lot of rows.

He had moved out the year before, for a while, and lived with his mother. Now, his girlfriend was again saying that she wanted him out.

He didn't want to go; he was desperate to make things work. But he couldn't understand what was wrong—she complained that he wasn't doing things and then, when he did do them, she was still unhappy. For instance, he said that she complained about the kitchen, so he cleaned the kitchen and she was still upset.

He said that he didn't think that she really knew what she was unhappy about. I commented that people often don't really know; they just know that something is wrong but are not sure what it is.

He worked long hours, and she also worked full-time. He wanted to make things work, but he complained that she picked fights all the time. Really, he said, it was all her fault; he was doing his best and she wasn't even trying.

Since they had the kids, they had no time together. They were both working, and although they had help from her parents during the day, they couldn't afford a babysitter so that they could go out on dates.

Every evening was dominated by getting the kids to bed and between that and the dogs and jobs round the house, they had no time.

I suggested that she could also be feeling neglected and unloved, and he agreed that she probably was. I explained Gottman's research and the behaviours that heal.

We looked at the positives. He still loved her and wanted to make things work. She knew he was seeing a counsellor and was interested to see if "it worked", which suggested there was still hope, although she refused to attend sessions.

He said that the last time she was on maternity leave, things between them had been much better which suggested that the fundamental problem was stress and a lack of time together.

We used relaxation and positive visualization to rehearse bringing in the three behaviours that heal.

Session 2—One week later

He had had a hard week. He had tried very hard and felt that everything had been thrown in his face. She had said some very harsh things to him, and he was very hurt.

He said that, no matter what he did, she focused only on what he had done wrong. They were rowing all the time, and it seemed to him that she was always looking to start a row or get a reaction.

Since she had been back at work, it had worsened. He said that he knew that he could be badly behaved too, and she was great a lot of the time, but her work seemed to make her worse.

Session 3—Two weeks later

He said they were being very polite to each other. He was really trying but saw no sign of change in her. They had decided to give it another six weeks and then, if there was no change, he had agreed to move out. He still felt that he couldn't win and that she found fault with everything he did. When he was affectionate, she asked, "Did the counsellor tell you to do that?"

We worked on his anger and lack of hope and did more positive visualization, which focused on building the loving future he wanted through continuing with the three behaviours that heal.

Session 4—One week later

Things have been up and down. He says the work on his anger "worked" and he has been much calmer. She still wants to row, and he doesn't—especially not in front of the kids.

He keeps forgetting his girlfriend's birthday. It is her birthday next month and she has told him that it is important to her. She wants him to remember and at least buy her a card. We discuss what he can do to get better at these things.

We talk about how they are using technology; he feels it is something that gets in the way of them talking more. We discuss strategies, including putting their phones away at home.

They have no landline so he says they can't switch off calls, but I suggest that they at least leave them at the door when they come in, turn off notifications and just check a couple of times, if anyone had rung.

We discuss the things they used to enjoy doing when they were first together and how they could bring more of those things back into their lives, now that they are a family. He plans to turn off the TV more and do things together instead.

Session 5—Two weeks later

I asked him how he was, and he said, "Good."

"Really?" I asked surprised.

"Yes, really! Everything has changed."

He tells me that they have been getting along well. They went to the beach with the kids at the weekend. It was fun and they held hands. They're back to sleeping together after more than a year.

We talked about the aim of creating a culture of appreciation in the home and the importance of not taking things personally. We rehearsed success some more.

Session 6—One month later

Everything was still going well.

Session 7—One month later

Everything was still going well, so we decided to make this the last session.

Case Study Two

Session 1

Nichola and Mark, a couple in their forties with one young child, had been married for four years and were having many rows. They were both working, Mark full-time and Nichola part-time and were thinking of splitting up.

For Mark, the main problem was a lack of sex. Nichola said that, for her, this was just a symptom of lots of other things that were wrong.

They also had some differences about how they raised their son. They came from very different families with different cultures and expectations about this.

We talked about child rearing and the different models and how practices and advice have changed. We also talked about their different family experiences and expectations and the advantages and disadvantages of different models.

I explained the importance of the three behaviours that heal, and we used relaxation and positive visualization to rehearse success.

Session 2—One week later

I saw Nichola on her own. She said that they'd felt that the first session had gone well. Nichola felt that her reluctance to have sex had to do with the relationship—that it was not going well.

She said that she would like to have a great sex life with Mark, but that was not how things were at the moment. She had had good and bad experiences of sex and felt that her bad experiences were still affecting her in the bedroom.

We did some work on putting her bad experiences into the past, using the Human Givens Rewind

Technique, and then some positive visualization of success.

Session 3—Two weeks later

Everything was still the same. I saw them together and Nichola talked about her frustrations with the relationship. Mark said that he was listening to Nichola more and appreciated that she had been feeling neglected for years. He said that he could see that she had withdrawn from the relationship.

Nichola said that there was pressure from her family, to do things in a certain way. They didn't approve of some of the things that Mark was doing. Nichola was supportive of her husband, but also shared some of her parent's concerns and we discussed this.

We talked again about attention and the three behaviours that heal and how they could make room for them in their busy lives. We also talked about stonewalling. Nichola felt that Mark did this, though Mark was not so sure.

We ended the session with more positive visualization focusing on creating a culture of appreciation in the home.

Session 4—Six weeks later

They had postponed an appointment because they had both been very busy and had also all been ill. Nichola felt frustrated that they had lost momentum because of this and that these days they only ever talked about childcare and housework; not anything more meaningful.

We talked about how their busy diaries left them with too little time for each other—they were always scheduling time for other people and activities but not for each other. They decided to start prioritising more time as a family and as a couple.

Nichola asked if she should force affection, if she didn't feel like it. I said no but explained that if other things—attention in particular—were worked on, affection would start to feel more natural.

Session 5—One month later

Things were going better. They had been playing cards and listening to music, after their son was in bed and going for walks with him rather than watching TV. They had been putting away their phones and had had sex for the first time in more than a year.

We also talked some more about their differences in raising their son.

Session 6—One month later

They had been away, as a family, for a wedding, and everything had gone well. They were getting along better. They now had a babysitter and were going out regularly together for walks and meals.

We had a long discussion about sexual intimacy and affection. Nichola felt that Mark always wanted affection to lead to sex. Mark felt that he would like more sex, but that he was always being rejected and that most of Nichola's affection and attention now went to their son.

Nichola said that she had never had an easy relationship with sex because of her upbringing. She found it difficult to talk about frankly, even with Mark.

I commented that this is a very common thing and we talked about the different messages that girls and boys and men and women get from society, in relation to sex.

I recommended some books and a website (see Further Information/Resources at the end of this book).

Session 7—One month later

Everything was the same as before. They were getting along better, but there was still no passion. Although, there was still hardly any affection between them, they both agreed that the tension that was there between them before, had gone.

Mark said that he couldn't see the relationship continuing for much longer without more regular sex. Nichola said that sex to her felt like an obligation now, and that that was a complete turn off.

I fed back to them that, at the root of their problems, there seemed to be a loss of emotional connection, which develops from a lack of expressions of affection and that this is very common.

Mark said that there was affection, but Nichola disagreed. She also stated that there was no romance. Mark said that he just wasn't very romantic.

We discussed romance and what that would look like. Nichola said that to her romance meant, flowers, candles, chocolates, kissing hello & goodbye, cards & gifts on special occasions and holding hands.

She also said that it was important to her that there was no expectation of sex in return for these things—for her that would kill all feeling of romance.

Mark struggled with how this would work. Nichola commented that they had been having difficulties in this area for years. We discussed this and how they could make it work in practice.

I suggested that Mark should hold off for at least the next month in any attempt to persuade Nichola to have sex, and instead, he should do more of the things we had discussed.

Nichola had been feeling hurt and neglected for a long time and I emphasised this to Mark. I suggested that he needed to put more effort into winning back her affection—in other words, to "court" her, like in the past.

I also suggested that he should see this as more like a marathon than a sprint because these things take time.

We ended with more positive visualization focusing on how they'd like to be.

Session 8—Two months later

They both said that they were getting along much better. Both felt that things were going well, that they had made lots of progress and that they were on the right track.

Nichola said that the way she felt and thought about sex and the whole relationship had changed for the positive. They both felt that they were getting there and that they were much happier together than before.

Mark said that he had had no hope of the therapy working, at the beginning and was amazed by the difference it had made.

We discussed the problems that they had been having when they first came to see me, and both said that they weren't having those problems or feeling that way anymore.

So, we agreed that this would be the last session, though they could book another session, at any time in the future, should they need it.

Conclusion

When a relationship is in difficulty, the most common advice people receive is to work on the communication. Unfortunately, that often leads to a focus on their problems and lots of stressful discussions.

For some couples, this can be counterproductive. It can lead to one partner increasingly avoiding the other, and, as a major contributing factor to their difficulties, is likely to be lack of attention, this avoidance can be disastrous.

Research shows that the form of communication that would really help, is listening, with your full attention, to whatever your partner wants to talk about.

The common-sense understanding that communication is important in relationships, is true; but the form that it most often needs to take, is listening to your partner talk about everyday stuff.

This is sometimes misunderstood to mean listening to your partner talk about their problems and concerns. But it is important to listen to them talk about everything and nothing!

For instance, their complaints but also the things that they are interested in and excited about—even it is just something they saw on the telly!

When this is done regularly over weeks, months, and years, it naturally leads to a good, in-depth understanding of what is truly important to your partner—what they enjoy doing, what they dislike, and what they value in life.

Happily, this is another thing that has been shown by the research, to be protective of a relationship; a good in-depth understanding of your partner and their world—and this follows on naturally from simply listening to your partner's daily preoccupations and concerns.

A proverb from the UK where I grew up is, "Look after the pennies and the pounds will look after themselves!"

This applies equally well to relationships. Look after the little things and the big things will often come right as well.

The little things matter. Get the little things right, and everything else will often follow.

In relationships, we can only work on ourselves — our own piece of the jigsaw.

Remember the Three Behaviours that Heal:

1) Attention (listening!)
2) Affection (make it a habit!)
3) Positive Focus (on what is good about your partner).

I created a mnemonic for you to make remembering this easier:

Attention and Affection makes Pals Forever!

So just do it— you know it makes sense!

Acknowledgments

With special thanks to The Gottman Institute, who carried out most of the research cited in this book, and generously gave me their permission to use it, and also to Joe Griffin and Ivan Tyrell for developing the wonderful, evidence-based Human Givens Therapy, without which I wouldn't have been able to write this book and without which I wouldn't be half as effective for my clients.

Also, thanks to Gary Williams, Sean Sumner, Chandler Bolt and Heidi Sutherlin who helped me to turn the dream of this book into reality. Not forgetting Nanci Hogan and Ann Walsh for regular support along the way, Jude Fay for early advice and encouragement, my editor Lizette Balsdon, and my friends, colleagues and many wonderful clients who have encouraged me to on this journey with all their positive feedback.

Also, special thanks go to my family, namely—Wieland, Esmie, and Jonas, Kathryn, Susan, Sarah, Dad, Enid, Kerstin, Brigitte and finally, my Mum, Florence Taylor, née Lynch—sadly gone, but not forgotten—for all their love and support over the years.

About the Author

Ann Marie Taylor is a Psychotherapist specialising in relationships. She studied Psychology at Bangor University in North Wales before gaining a distinction in Human Givens Therapy (HGT) in 2002. Ann Marie has worked professionally with people in distress for more than thirty years.

Ann Marie combined key findings from Professor John Gottman's 40 years of research on relationships with methods from HGT, to develop her own evidence-based method of working with couples in distress. She has found it to be very effective in helping people turn around struggling relationships.

Human Givens Therapy is a brief, solution-focused psychotherapy based on an up to date, understanding of the mind/body system from psychology and neurobiology.

It combines several approaches to maximising well-being including performance-enhancing & motivational techniques, and draws on ancient wisdom, in its use of stories and metaphors.

Ann Marie was born & brought up in East Yorkshire, UK and is the eldest of four sisters. She lives in County Wicklow, Ireland between the mountains and the sea, with her husband & teenage children. This is her first book.

Notes and Reference

1) TED Talk by Robert Waldinger, Director of the Harvard Study of Adult Development, one of the most comprehensive longitudinal studies in history. https://www.ted.com/talks/robert_waldinger_what_makes_a_good_life_lessons_from_the_longest_study_on_happiness?language=en

2) For more detail on Gottman's research methods - see https://www.gottman.com/about/research

3) The Relationship Cure by John Gottman & Joan DeClaire, 3-4.

4) Human Givens: The New Approach to Emotional Health and Clear Thinking by Ivan Tyrrell & Joe Griffin, 61-62.

5) Emotional Intelligence by Daniel Goleman, Chapter 2: Anatomy of an emotional hijacking

6) Turning away (no response or an unrelated response) was found to be the most harmful response to a bid for connection.

7) Multiple sources including: www.historyanswers.co.uk

8) Emotional Intelligence by Daniel Goleman, Chapter 2: Anatomy of an emotional hijacking.

9) John Gottman in The Truth about Great Relationships, YouTube

10) In Search of Solutions: A New Direction in Psychotherapy by Bill O'Hanlon, Michele Weiner-Davis

11) The Seven Principles for Making Marriage Work, John Gottman, Chapter 4, Principle 1: Enhance Your Love Maps

12) The Seven Principles for Making Marriage Work, John Gottman; chapter 3, How I Predict Divorce (pg37).

13) You Just Don't Understand: Women and Men in Conversation Deborah Tannen She argues that for most women" the language of conversation is primarily a language of rapport: a way of establishing connections and negotiating relationships" while for most men , by contrast, " talk is primarily a means to preserve independence and negotiate and maintain status in a hierarchical social order" (pg77).

14) The essential innate emotional needs and resources were first collated from the research literature by Ivan Tyrrell & Joe Griffin. Human Givens: A New Approach to Emotional Health and Clear Thinking by Ivan Tyrrell & Joe Griffin.

15) Ibid.

16) https://www.gottman.com/blog/building-great-sex-life-not-rocket-science/

17) For example, The Sexualization of Girls: An Update. Prepared for Culture Reframed – published January 2019 cultureframed.org

18) John Gottman in The Truth about Great Relationships, YouTube https://m.youtube.com/watch?v=WRobpAKT7Qs

19) The Emotional Brain: the Mysterious Underpinnings of Emotional Life by Joseph Le Doux, Phoenix.

20) Human Givens: The New Approach to Emotional Health and Clear Thinking by Ivan Tyrrell & Joe Griffin,154-166

21) For example, Increased psychosocial strain in Lithuanian versus Swedish men (the LiVicordia Study) https://www.ncbi.nlm.nih.gov/pubmed/9625214

22) The Emotional Brain: the Mysterious Underpinnings of Emotional Life by Joseph Le Doux, Phoenix, 240-246.

23) Cigarettes https://www.ncbi.nlm.nih.gov/pubmed/7086634

24) Hold me tight, Seven Conversations for a Lifetime of Love by Dr Sue Johnson, Little Brown.

Further Reading/Resources

Relationships

Website: https://www.gottman.com/

The Relationship Cure: A 5 Step Guide for Building Better Connections with Family, Friends and Lovers by John M. Gottman

The Seven Principles for making marriage work-John Gottman and Nan Silver

Why Marriages Succeed or Fail—and how to make yours last by John Gottman

How to Complain without Hurting your Partner: https://m.youtube.com/watch?v=bShsyKUFjKE

Making Relationships Work: https://m.youtube.com/watch?v=LLXX8wzvT7c

The Five Love Languages by Gary Chapman

Human Givens

Website: https://www.hgi.org.uk/

Emotional Needs Audit:
https://www.hgi.org.uk/sites/default/files/hgi/Emotional-Needs-Audit.pdf

Human Givens: The New Approach to Emotional Health and Clear Thinking by Ivan Tyrrell and Joe Griffin

Why we dream: The definitive answer by Joe Griffin, Ivan Tyrrell

How to lift depression ... Fast (The Human Givens Approach Book 1) by Joe Griffin, Ivan Tyrrell

How to master anxiety by Joe Griffin, Ivan Tyrrell

The Brain

The Emotional Brain by Joseph Le Doux

Synaptic Self: how our brains become who we are by Joseph Le Doux

Emotional Intelligence by Daniel Goleman

Communication

You Just Don't Understand: Women and Men in Conversation by Deborah Tannen

I Hear You by: The Surprisingly Simple Skill Behind Extraordinary Relationships by Michael S. Sorensen

Relaxation

Digital download: https://www.human-givens.com/publications/relax/

Sex

Article on how to have great sex: https://www.gottman.com/blog/building-great-sex-life-not-rocket-science/

Come as You Are: the surprising new science that will transform your sex life by Emily Nagoski

She Comes First: The Thinking Man's Guide to Pleasuring a Woman by Ian Kerner

Becoming Orgasmic: A sexual and personal growth programme for women by Julia R. Heiman and Joseph LoPiccolo

Website (WARNING- explicit information on all forms of sex):

http://dodsonandross.com/

Therapy

In Search of Solutions: a new direction in psychotherapy by William Hudson O'Hanlon and Michele Weiner Davis

Human Givens— An Idea in Practice: using the human givens approach edited by Joe Griffin and Ivan Tyrrell

101 Healing Stories: using metaphors in therapy by George W. Burns

Transforming Tales: how stories can change people by Rob Parkinson

One final thing...

Thank you for reading my book!

I hope you found it helpful & enjoyable.

My purpose in writing this book was to bring the most useful but little-known, findings of the research to as wide an audience as possible, in a way that is easy to understand.

If you liked my book, you could help me to meet this aim by leaving a review on Amazon.

https://www.amazon.com/dp/B081Z1LR9Q

Your feedback will help me to reach more people as well as, improve the next edition, and any future books.

Thank you!

Printed in Poland
by Amazon Fulfillment
Poland Sp. z o.o., Wrocław

53384850R00108